T0147012

PANEGYRIC

Radical Thinkers ▼

PANEGYRIC

Volumes 1 & 2

Guy Debord

Volume 1 translated by James Brook

Volume 2 translated by John McHale

VERSO

London • New York

Volume 1 first published by Éditions Gérard Lebovici, Paris 1989
Volume 2 first published by Librairie Arthème Fayard, Paris 1997
© Éditions Gallimard 1993

This edition first published by Verso 2004
© Verso 2004
Reprinted 2009
Revised translation of Volume 1 © James Brook 2004;
based on a previous translation © James Brook 1991
Translation of Volume 2 © John McHale 2004
All rights reserved

3 5 7 9 10 8 6 4 2

Verso
UK: 6 Meard Street, London W1F 0EG
US: 388 Atlantic Ave, Brooklyn, NY 11217
www.versobooks.com

Verso is the imprint of New Left Books

ISBN-13: 978-1-84467-353-7

British Library Cataloguing in Publication Data
A catalogue record for this book is available from the British Library

Library of Congress Cataloging-in-Publication Data
A catalog record for this book is available from the Library of Congress

Printed in the US

CONTENTS

Panegyric

VOLUME 1

GUY DEBORD

Translated by James Brook

I am very grateful to Malcolm Imrie, Ken Knabb,
John McHale, and Donald Nicholson-Smith
for their help on this revision of my 1991
translation. Errors remain the responsibility
of the foolhardy translator.

James Brook
San Francisco, 2004.

'*Panegyric* expresses more than eulogy. *Eulogy* no doubt includes praise of the person, but it does not exclude a certain criticism, a certain blame. *Panegyric* entails neither blame nor criticism.'

LITTRÉ, *Dictionnaire de la langue française.*

'Why ask me of my lineage? Men come and go as leaves year by year upon the trees. Those of autumn the wind sheds upon the ground, but when the season of spring returns the forest buds forth with fresh vines. Even so is it with the generations of humankind, the new spring up as the old are passing away.'

Iliad, Book VI.

I

'As to his plan, we flatter ourselves we can demonstrate that he has none – that he writes almost at random, mingling facts and bringing them together without connexion or order; confounding the affairs of one epoch with those belonging to another; disdaining to justify his accusations or eulogies; adopting without examination, and without that critical spirit so necessary to the historian, the false judgments of prejudice, of rivalry or of enmity, and the exaggerations of spite or bad feeling; attributing actions to some, and language to others, incompatible with their stations and characters; never quoting any witness but himself, nor better authority than his own assertions.'

GENERAL GOURGAUD,
Napoleon and the Grand Army in Russia; or, A Critical Examination of Count Philip de Ségur's Work.

ALL MY LIFE I have seen only troubled times, extreme divisions in society, and immense destruction; I have taken part in these troubles. Such circumstances would doubtless suffice to prevent the most transparent of my acts or thoughts from ever being universally approved. But in addition, I do believe, several of them may have been misunderstood.

Clausewitz, at the beginning of his history of the campaign of 1815, gives this summary of his method: 'In every strategical critique, the essential thing is to put oneself exactly in the position of the actors; it is true that this is often very difficult.' The difficult thing is to know 'all the circumstances in which the actors found themselves' at a given moment, in order to be in a position to judge soundly their series of choices in the conduct of their war: how they did what they did and what they might have been able to do differently. So it is necessary to know what they wanted, above all, and, of course, what they believed, without forgetting what they did not know. And what they did not know then was not only the result yet to come of their own operations clashing with the operations that were pitted against them, but also much of what was already weighing against them, in the disposition or strength of the enemy camp, but which remained hidden from them. And basically they did not know the exact value to accord to their own forces, until these could make their value known at the actual moment of their employment, whose outcome, moreover, sometimes changes that value just as much as it tests it.

A person who has led an action, the great consequences of which were felt at a distance, has often been nearly alone in his knowledge of some rather important aspects, which various reasons have encouraged him to keep hidden, while other aspects have since been forgotten, simply because those times have passed or the people who were familiar with those aspects are dead. And even the testimony of the living is not always accessible. One person does not really know how to write; another is held back by more current interests or ambitions; a third may be afraid; and yet another might be worried about his reputation. As will be seen, I am not hindered by any of these impediments. Speaking, then, as coolly as possible about things that have aroused so much passion, I am going to say what I have done. Assuredly, a great many, if not all, unjust rebukes will find themselves immediately swept away like dust. And I am convinced that the broad lines of the history of my times will stand out more clearly.

I will be obliged to go into some detail. That could take me rather a long way; I do not deny the magnitude of the task. I will take whatever time is necessary. Even so, I will not say, as Sterne did when beginning to write *The Life and Opinions of Tristram Shandy*, that I am resolved 'not to be in a hurry – but to go on leisurely, writing and publishing two volumes of my life every year ... if I am suffered to go on quietly, and can make a tolerable bargain with my bookseller.' For I certainly do not want to commit myself to publishing two volumes a year or even promise any less precipitous rhythm.

My method will be very simple. I will tell what I have loved; and, in this light, everything else will become evident and make itself well enough understood.

'Deceitful time hides its traces from us, but it goes swiftly by,' writes the poet Li Po, who adds:

'Perhaps you still retain youth's light heart / but your hair is already white; and what use is complaining?' I don't intend to complain about anything, and certainly not about the way I have been able to live.

Much less do I wish to hide its traces, which I know to be exemplary. Because of the subject's many difficulties, it has always been rare for someone to set out to give a precise account of what the life he has known actually was. And this will be perhaps even more precious now, in an era when so many things have been changed at the astounding speed of catastrophes, in an era about which one can say that almost every point of reference and comparison has suddenly been swept away, along with the very ground on which the old society was built.

In any case, it is easy for me to be sincere. I find nothing that can cause me the least embarrassment on any subject. I never believed in the received values of my contemporaries, and today no one takes cognizance of any of them. Perhaps still too scrupulous, Lacenaire exaggerated, it seems to me, the responsibility he had directly incurred in the violent deaths of a very small number of people: 'Even with the blood that covers me, I think I'm worth more than most of the men I've met,' he wrote to Jacques Arago. ('But you were there with us, Monsieur Arago, on the barricades in 1832. Remember the Cloître Saint-Merry... You don't know what poverty is, Monsieur Arago. You've never been hungry,' the workers on the June 1848 barricades were soon to answer not him but his brother, who had come to harangue them like a Roman on the iniquity of rebelling against the laws of the Republic.)

There is nothing more natural than to consider everything from the standpoint of oneself, taken as the centre of the world; one finds oneself thus capable of condemning the world without even bothering to hear its deceitful chatter. One need only mark off the precise limits that necessarily restrict this authority: one's own place in the course of time and in society; what one has done and what one has known, one's dominant passions. 'Who, then, can write the truth better than the man who has experienced it?' The author of the most beautiful memoirs of the seventeenth century, who has not escaped the inept reproach of having spoken of his conduct without maintaining the appearance of the coldest objectivity, was the one who made that apt observation concerning truth, which he supported by quoting the opinion of the Président de Thou, according to whom 'there are no true histories but those written by men who have been sufficiently sincere to speak truly about themselves.'

Some might be surprised that I implicitly seem to compare myself, here and there, on a point of detail, with some great mind of the past or simply with personalities who have been noticed by history. They would be wrong. I do not claim to resemble any other person, and I believe that the present era is little comparable to the past. But many figures of the past, in all their extreme diversity, are still quite commonly known. They represent, in brief, a readily accessible index of human behaviour or propensities. Those who may not know who they were can easily find out; and the ability to make oneself understood is always a virtue in a writer.

I will have to make rather extensive use of quotations. Never, I believe, to lend authority to a particular argument but only to show fully of what stuff this adventure and I are made. Quotations are useful in periods of ignorance or obscurantist beliefs. Allusions, without quotation marks, to other texts known to be very famous, as in classical Chinese poetry, Shakespeare, or Lautréamont, should be reserved for times richer in minds capable of recognizing the original phrase and the distance its new application has introduced. Today, when irony itself is not always understood, there is the risk of the phrase being confidently attributed to oneself and, moreover, being hastily and incorrectly reproduced. The antique ponderousness of exact quotation will be compensated for, I hope, by the quality of the selections. They will appear when appropriate in this text: no computer could have provided me with this pertinent variety.

Those who wish to write quickly a piece about nothing that no one will read through even once, whether in a newspaper or a book, confidently extol the style of the spoken language, because they find it much easier, more modern and direct. They themselves do not know how to speak. Neither do their readers, the language actually spoken under modern conditions of life having been socially reduced to a mere representation of itself, as endorsed by the media, and comprising some six or eight constantly repeated turns of phrase and fewer than two hundred terms, most of them neologisms, with a turnover of a third of them every six months. All this favours a certain hasty solidarity. In contrast, I for my part am going to write without affectation or fatigue, as the most natural and easiest thing in the world, in the language I have learned and, in most circumstances, spoken. It's not up to me to change it. The Gypsies rightly contend that one is never obliged to speak the truth except in one's own language; in the enemy's language the lie must reign. Another advantage: by referring to the vast corpus of classic texts that have appeared in French throughout the five centuries before my birth, but especially in the last two, it will always be easy to properly translate me into any future idiom, even when French has become a dead language.

In our century, who could fail to be aware that a person who finds it in his interest to instantly affirm any sort of nonsense will say it any which way? The immense increase in the means of modern domination has so marked the style of its pronouncements that if the understanding of the development of the dismal argumentations of power was for a long time a privilege of people of real intelligence, it has now inevitably become familiar to even the most dull-witted. It is in this sense that the truth of this report on my times may be rather well demonstrated by its style. The tone of this discourse will in itself be sufficient guarantee, for everyone will understand that it is only by dint of having lived in such a way that one can have the expertise for this kind of account.

It is known for certain that the Peloponnesian War took place. But it is only through Thucydides that we know of its implacable development and its lessons. No cross-checking is possible; nor was it necessary, because the veracity of the facts, like the coherence of the thought, was so well impressed upon his contemporaries and near posterity that any other witness felt discouraged when faced with the difficulty of introducing a different interpretation of the events or even quibbling over a detail.

In the same way, I believe people will have to rest content with the history I am now going to present. Because no one, for a long time to come, will have the audacity to undertake to demonstrate, on any aspect, the contrary of what I will say, whether it be a matter of finding the slightest inexact element in the facts or of maintaining another point of view on them.

Conventional as this procedure might be judged, I think, first of all, that it will not be useless here to clearly sketch out the beginning: the date and the general conditions under which began a story that I will not fail to abandon subsequently to all the confusion demanded by its theme. It is reasonable to think that many things first appear in youth, to stay with you for a long while. I was born in 1931, in Paris. Just then, my family's fortune was shattered by the consequences of the world economic crisis that had first appeared in America a little earlier; and the remnants did not seem capable of lasting much beyond my majority, which in fact is what happened. So I was born virtually ruined. I was not, strictly speaking, unaware of the fact that I should not expect an inheritance, and in the end I did not receive one. I simply did not grant the slightest importance to those rather abstract questions about the future. Thus, throughout the course of my adolescence, I moved slowly but inevitably towards a life of adventure, eyes open – if indeed it can be said that my eyes were open on this question as well as on most others. I could not even think of studying for any of the scholarly qualifications needed to obtain employment, for all of them seemed alien to my tastes or contrary to my opinions. The people I respected more than anyone in the world were Arthur Cravan and Lautréamont, and I knew perfectly well that all their friends, if I had consented to pursue university studies, would have despised me as much as if I had resigned myself to exercising an artistic activity; and if I could not have had those friends, I certainly would not have stooped to consoling myself with others. A doctor of nothing, I firmly kept myself apart from all semblance of participation in the circles that then passed for intellectual or artistic. I admit that my merit in this respect was well tempered by my great laziness, as well as by my very meagre capacities for confronting the work of such careers.

Never to have given more than very slight attention to questions of money, and absolutely none to the ambition of holding some brilliant post in society, is a trait so rare among my contemporaries that some will no doubt consider it incredible, even in my case. It is, however, true, and it has been so constantly and abidingly verifiable that the public will just have to get used to it. I imagine that the cause resided in the fact that my carefree upbringing encountered favourable terrain. I never saw any bourgeois at work, with the baseness that their special kind of work inevitably entails; and perhaps that is the reason why in this indifference I was able to learn something about life, but, all told, solely through absence or by default. The moment of decadence of any form of social superiority is doubtless rather more amiable than its vulgar beginnings. I remain attached to this preference, which I had felt very early on, and I can say that poverty has principally given me a great deal of leisure, since I had no ruined properties to manage or dreams of restoring them through participation in the government of the state. It is true that I have tasted pleasures little known to people who have obeyed the lamentable laws of this era. It is also true that I have strictly observed several duties of which they have not the slightest idea. 'For you see only the external husk of our life,' *The Rule of the Templars* stated bluntly in its time, 'but you do not know the severe commandments within.' I should also note, to cite all the favourable influences met with in my youth, the obvious fact that I had the opportunity to read several good books, from which it is always possible to find by oneself all the others, or even to write those that are still lacking. This quite complete account will break off here.

Before the age of twenty I saw the peaceful part of my youth draw to a close; and I now had no further obligation than to pursue all my tastes without restraint, albeit under difficult conditions. I headed first of all towards that very alluring milieu where an extreme nihilism no longer had any interest in knowing about or continuing any previously accepted way of life or use of the arts. This milieu readily recognized me as one of its own. Thus disappeared my last possibilities of one day returning to the normal round of existence. I thought so then, and what came after proved it.

I must be less inclined than others to calculate, since that choice, which was made so quickly and which committed me to so much, was spontaneous, the product of a heedlessness on which I have never gone back; and which later, having had the leisure in which to judge its consequences, I have never regretted. It might easily be said that in terms of wealth or reputation I had nothing to lose; but, after all, neither had I anything to gain.

This milieu of demolition experts, more distinctly than its precursors of the two or three preceding generations, was then very closely associated with the dangerous classes. When one lives with them, one ends up to a great degree living their kind of life. Enduring traces of this obviously remain. Over the years, more than half the people I knew well had sojourned one or more times in the prisons of various countries; many, no doubt, for political reasons, but all the same a greater number for common-law offences or crimes. So I met mainly rebels and poor people. I saw around me a great many individuals who would die young, and not always by suicide, frequent though that was. Regarding violent death, I will note, without being able to put forward a fully rational explanation of the phenomenon, that the number of my friends who have been killed by bullets constitutes an uncommonly high percentage, leaving aside military operations, of course.

Our only public activities, which remained rare and brief in the early years, were meant to be completely unacceptable: at first, primarily due to their form; later, as they acquired depth, primarily due to their content. They were not accepted. 'Destruction was my Beatrice,' wrote Mallarmé, who was himself the guide for a few others in rather perilous explorations. It is quite certain that whoever devotes himself exclusively to making such historical demonstrations, and thus refuses all available work, has to know how to live off the land. I will discuss the question in considerably more detail later on. Confining myself here to presenting the subject at its most general, I will say that I have always made a point of giving the vague impression that I had great intellectual, even artistic, qualities of which I preferred to deprive my era, which did not seem to deserve to use them. There have always been people to regret this absence and, paradoxically, to help me maintain it. If this has turned out well, it is only because I have never sought out anyone, anywhere. My entourage has been composed only of those who came of their own accord and were capable of getting themselves accepted. Has even one other person dared to behave like me, in this era? It must also be acknowledged that the degradation of all existing conditions occurred at precisely the same moment, as if to justify my singular folly.

I must likewise admit, for nothing can remain purely unalterable in the course of time, that after some twenty years or so an advanced fraction of a specialized public seemed to begin to no longer completely reject the idea that I might have several genuine talents, talents that were especially remarkable in comparison with the great poverty of the trivial discoveries and pointless repetitions that those people had for so long felt worthy of admiration, and this despite the fact that the only discernible use of my gifts had to be regarded as entirely nefarious. And then, of course, it was I who refused to agree, in any way, to recognize the existence of these people who were beginning, so to speak, to recognize something of mine. It is true that they were not ready to accept everything, and I have always clearly stated that it would be all or nothing, thus placing myself definitively out of reach of their possible concessions. In regard to society, my tastes and ideas have not changed, remaining as strictly opposed to what it was as to all that it claimed to want to become.

The leopard dies with its spots, and I have never intended to improve myself or believed myself capable of doing so. I have never really aspired to any sort of virtue, except perhaps to that of having thought that only a few crimes of a new type, which could certainly not have been cited in the past, might not be unworthy of me; and to that of not having changed, after such a bad start. At a critical moment in the troubles of the Fronde, Gondi, who had given such sterling proofs of his capacities in the handling of human affairs, notably in his favourite role of disturber of the public peace, improvised successfully before the Parlement de Paris a fine quotation attributed to a classical author, for whose name everyone vainly searched, but which could best be applied to his own panegyric: '*In difficillimis Reipublicae temporibus, urbem non deserui; in prosperis nihil de publico delibavi; in desperatis, nihil timui.*' He himself translated it like this: 'In bad times I did not forsake the city; in prosperous times I had no private interests; in desperate times I feared nothing.'

II

'These were the things done in this winter. And so ended the second year of this war, written by Thucydides.'

THUCYDIDES, *The Peloponnesian War.*

IN THE quartier of perdition where my youth went as if to complete its education, one might have said that the portents of an imminent collapse of the whole edifice of civilization had a rendezvous. Permanently ensconced there were people who could be defined only negatively, for the good reason that they had no trade, followed no course of study, and practised no art. Many of them had participated in the recent wars, in several of the armies that had fought over the continent: the German, the French, the Russian, the American, the two Spanish armies, and several others. The remainder, who were five or six years younger, had come there directly, because the idea of the family had begun to dissolve, like all others. No received doctrine moderated anyone's conduct, much less offered

their existence any illusory goal. Various practices of the moment were always ready to present,
in light of the evidence, their ready defence.
Nihilism is quick to moralize, as soon as it is
touched by the idea of self-justification: one man
robbed banks and took pride in not robbing the
poor, while another had never killed anyone when
he was not angry. Despite all the eloquence at
their disposal, they were the most unpredictable
people from one hour to the next, and they were
sometimes quite dangerous. It is the fact of
having passed through such a milieu that later
permitted me to say sometimes, with the same
pride as the demagogue in Aristophanes' *Knights*:
'I too grew up in the streets!'

After all, it was modern poetry, for the last
hundred years, that had led us there. We were a
handful who thought it necessary to carry out its
programme in reality, and certainly to do nothing
else. People have sometimes been surprised – to
tell the truth, only since an extremely recent date
– to discover the atmosphere of hate and maledic-
tion that has constantly surrounded me and, as
much as possible, kept me concealed. Some think
it is because of the grave responsibility that has
often been attributed to me for the origins, or even
for the command, of the May 1968 revolt. I think
rather it is what I did in 1952 that has been

disliked for so long. An angry queen of France once reminded her most seditious subject: 'There is rebellion in imagining that one could rebel.'

That is just what happened. Another, earlier contemner of the world, who said he had been a king in Jerusalem, had touched on the heart of the problem, almost with these very words: The spirit whirleth about continually, and the spirit returneth again according to its circuits. All revolutions run into history, yet history is not full; unto the place from whence the rivers of revolution come, thither they return again.

There have always been artists or poets capable of living in violence. The impatient Marlowe died, knife in hand, arguing over a tavern bill. It is generally thought that Shakespeare was thinking of the death of his rival when he made, without too much fear of being reproached for heavy-handedness, this joke in *As You Like It*: 'it strikes a man more dead than a great reckoning in a little room.' This time, what was an absolutely new phenomenon, which naturally left few traces, was that the sole principle accepted by all was precisely that there could be no more poetry or art – and that something better had to be found.

We had several features in common with those other devotees of the dangerous life who had spent their time, exactly five hundred years before us, in the same city and on the same bank of the river. Obviously, I cannot be compared to someone who has mastered his art like François Villon. And I was not as irremediably engaged as he in organized crime; nor had I studied so well at any university. But there was that 'noble man' among my friends who was the complete equal of Régnier de Montigny, as well as many other rebels destined for bad ends; and the pleasures and splendour of those lost young hoodlum girls who kept us such good company in our dives must not have been so very different from the girls those others had known under the names of Marion l'Idole or Catherine, Biétrix, and Bellet. I will speak of what we were then in the argot of Villon's accomplices, which is certainly no longer an impenetrable secret language. On the contrary, it is generally accessible to people in the know. But I will thus put the inevitable criminological dimension at a reassuring philological distance:

There I stagged a few kiddies the switcher was waiting for: prigs and millers. They were mobs you could trust, for they stood no repairs when it came to ramping. They were often limed by the reelers, but they were good at slanging innocent and tipping them rum gammon. That's where I learned how to chaff cross-kidders, so that long after, and even now, I'd rather keep dubber-mummed about such lays. Our hustling and our rigs are past. And yet I vividly remember my schoolmen down on the knuckle who piped so rummy this cracked world, when all of us met up in our regular patter-cribs, at Paris in darkmans.

I pride myself on having neither forgotten nor learnt anything in this regard. There were cold streets and snow, and the river in flood: 'In the middle of the bed / the river runs deep.' There were the girls who had run away from school, with their proud eyes and sweet lips; the frequent police searches; the roar of the cataract of time. 'Never again will we drink so young.'

One could say that I have always loved foreign women. From Hungary and Spain, from China and Germany, from Russia and Italy came those who filled my youth with joy. And later, when my hair was already grey, I lost what little reason the long course of time had perhaps, with great difficulty, succeeded in granting me, for a girl from Córdoba. Omar Khayyám, having given the matter some thought, had to admit: 'Indeed the Idols I have loved so long / Have done my credit in this World much wrong: / Have drowned my Glory in a shallow Cup, / And sold my Reputation for a Song.' Who better than I could appreciate the soundness of this observation?

But also, who as much as I has scorned all the valuations of my era and the reputations it awarded? The outcome was already contained in the beginning of this journey.

And that took place between the autumn of 1952 and the spring of 1953, in Paris, south of the Seine and north of Rue de Vaugirard, east of the Carrefour de la Croix-Rouge, and west of Rue Dauphine. Archilochus wrote, 'Come, go then with a cup ... draw drink from the hollow tuns, draining the red wine to the lees; for we no more than other men can stay sober on this watch.'

Somewhere between Rue du Four and Rue de Buci, where our youth was so completely lost, as a few glasses were drunk, one could feel certain that we would never do anything better.

III

'I have noticed that most of those who have left us their memoirs have recorded their bad actions and inclinations only when, as does sometimes happen, they have mistaken them for brave deeds or worthy instincts.'

ALEXIS DE TOCQUEVILLE, *Recollections.*

AFTER the circumstances I have just recalled, it is undoubtedly the rapidly acquired habit of drinking that has most marked my entire life. Wines, spirits, and beers: the moments when some of them became essential and the moments when they returned have marked out the main course and the meanders of days, weeks, years. Two or three other passions, of which I will speak, have been more or less continuously important in my life. But drinking has been the most constant and the most present. Among the small number of things that I have liked and known how to do well, what I have assuredly known how to do best is drink. Although I have read a lot, I have drunk even more. I have written much less than most people who write, but I have drunk much more than most people who drink. I can count myself among those of whom Baltasar Gracián, thinking about an elite discernible only among the Germans – but here he was quite unjust to the detriment of the French, as I think I have shown – could say, 'There are those who got drunk only once, but that once lasted them a lifetime.'

Furthermore, I am a little surprised, I who have had to read so often the most extravagant calumnies or quite unjust criticisms of myself, to see that in fact thirty or more years have passed without some malcontent ever instancing my drunkenness as at least an implicit argument against my scandalous ideas – with the one, belated exception of a piece by some young English drug addicts who revealed around 1980 that I was stupefied by drink and thus no longer harmful. I never for a moment dreamed of concealing this perhaps questionable side of my personality, and it was clearly evident for all those who met me more than once or twice. I can even note that on each occasion it sufficed but a few days for me to be highly esteemed, in Venice as in Cadiz, in Hamburg as in Lisbon, by the people I met only by frequenting certain cafés.

At first, like everyone, I appreciated the effect of mild drunkenness; then very soon I grew to like what lies beyond violent drunkenness, once that

stage is past: a terrible and magnificent peace, the
true taste of the passage of time. Although in the
first decades I may have allowed only slight indi-
cations to appear once or twice a week, I was, in
fact, continuously drunk for periods of several
months; and the rest of the time, I still drank a lot.

An air of disorder in the great variety of
emptied bottles remains susceptible, all the same,
to an a posteriori classification. First, I can distin-
guish between the drinks I consumed in their
countries of origin and those I consumed in Paris;
but almost every variety of drink was to be had in
mid-century Paris. Everywhere, the premises can
be subdivided simply between what I drank at
home, or at friends', or in cafés, cellars, bars,
restaurants, or in the streets, notably on café
terraces.

The hours and their shifting conditions almost
always retain a decisive role in the necessary
renewal of the stages of a binge, and each brings
its reasonable preference to bear on the available
possibilities. There is what one drinks in the
mornings, and for quite a long while that was the
time for beer. In *Cannery Row* a character who
one can tell is a connoisseur proclaims, 'There's
nothing like that first taste of beer.' But often
upon waking I have needed Russian vodka. There
is what is drunk with meals, and in the afternoons

that stretch out between them. At night, there is wine, along with spirits; later on, beer is welcome again, for then beer makes you thirsty. There is what one drinks at the end of the night, at the moment when the day begins anew. One can imagine that all this has left me very little time for writing, and that is exactly as it should be: writing should remain a rare thing, since one must have drunk for a long time before finding excellence.

I have wandered extensively in several great European cities, and I appreciated everything that deserved appreciation. The catalogue on this subject could be vast. There were the beers of England, where mild and bitter were mixed in pints; the big schooners of Munich; the Irish beers; and the most classical, the Czech beer of Pilsen; and the admirable baroque character of the Gueuze around Brussels, when it had its distinctive flavour in each local brewery and did not travel well. There were the fruit brandies of Alsace; the rum of Jamaica; the punches, the aquavit of Aalborg, and the grappa of Turin, cognac, cocktails; the incomparable mezcal of Mexico. There were all the wines of France, the loveliest coming from Burgundy; there were the wines of Italy, especially the Barolos of the Langhe and the Chiantis of Tuscany; there were the wines of Spain, the Riojas of Old Castille or the Jumilla of Murcia.

I would have had very few illnesses if drink had not in the end caused me some, from insomnia to gout to vertigo. 'Beautiful as the tremor of the hands in alcoholism,' said Lautréamont. There are mornings that are stirring but difficult.

'It is better to hide one's folly, but that is difficult in debauchery or drunkenness,' Heraclitus thought. And yet Machiavelli would write to Francesco Vettori: 'Anyone reading our letters ... would sometimes think that we are serious people entirely devoted to great things, that our hearts cannot conceive any thought which is not honourable and grand. But then, as these same people turned the page, we would seem thoughtless, inconstant, lascivious, entirely devoted to vanities. And even if someone judges this way of life shameful, I find it praiseworthy, for we imitate nature, which is changeable.' Vauvenargues formulated a rule too often forgotten: 'In order to decide that an author contradicts himself, it must be impossible to conciliate him.'

Moreover, some of my reasons for drinking are respectable. Like Li Po, I can indeed exhibit this noble satisfaction: 'For thirty years, I've hidden my fame in taverns.'

The majority of the wines, almost all the spirits, and every one of the beers whose memory I have evoked here have today completely lost their tastes, first on the world market and then locally, with the progress of industry as well as the disappearance or economic re-education of the social classes that had long remained independent of large industrial production; and thus also through the interplay of the various government regulations that now prohibit virtually anything that is not industrially produced. The bottles, so that they can still be sold, have faithfully retained their labels; this attention to detail gives the assurance that one can photograph them as they used to be – but not drink them.

Neither I nor the people who drank with me have at any moment felt embarrassed by our excesses. 'At the banquet of life' – good guests there, at least – we took a seat without thinking even for an instant that what we were drinking with such prodigality would not subsequently be replenished for those who would come after us. In drinking memory, no one had ever imagined that he would see drink pass away before the drinker.

IV

' 'Tis true, Julius Caesar wrote his own Commentaries; but then that Hero's Modesty in his Commentaries is equal to his Bravery: He seems to have undertaken that Work only, that he might have no Room for Flattery to impose upon future Ages in the Matter of his History.'

BALTASAR GRACIÁN, *The Compleat Gentleman.*

I HAVE known the world quite well, then, its history and geography, its landscapes and those who populated them, their various practices and, particularly, 'what sovereignty is, how many kinds there are, how one acquires it, how one keeps it, how one loses it.'

I have had no need to travel very far, but I have considered things with a certain thoroughness, according each the full measure of months or years it seemed to merit. The greater part of the time I lived in Paris; specifically, within the triangle defined by the intersections of Rue Saint-Jacques and Rue Royer-Collard, Rue Saint-Martin and Rue Greneta, and Rue du Bac and Rue de Commailles. Indeed, I spent my days and nights in this limited space and the narrow border zone that is its immediate extension – most often on its eastern side, more rarely on its north-western side.

Never, or hardly ever, would I have left this area, which suited me perfectly, if a few histor-ical necessities had not several times obliged me to do so. Always briefly in my youth, when I had to hazard some forays abroad to further extend disruption; but later on for much longer, when the city had been sacked and the kind of life that had been led there had been completely destroyed. Which is what happened from 1970 on.

I believe that this city was ravaged a little before all the others because its ever-renewed revolutions had so worried and shocked the world; and because, unfortunately, they had always failed. So we have been punished with a destruction as complete as that which had been threatened earlier by the Brunswick Manifesto or the speech of the Girondist Isnard: the aim was to bury so many fearsome memories and the great name of Paris. (The despicable Isnard, pre-siding over the Convention in May 1793, had already had the impudence to announce prema-turely: 'I say that if through these incessant insurrections the nation's representatives should happen to be attacked – I declare to you, in the name of all France, *Paris would be annihilated; soon one would have to search the banks of the Seine to determine whether the city ever existed.'*)

To see the banks of the Seine is to see our grief: nothing is found there now save the bustling columns of an anthill of motorized slaves. The historian Guicciardini, who lived through the end of the freedom of Florence, noted in his *Ricordi*: 'All cities, all states, all reigns are mortal. Everything, either by nature or by accident, ends at some time. And so a citizen who is living in the final stage of his country's existence should not feel as sorry for his country as he should for himself. What happened to his country was inevitable; but to be born at a time when such a disaster had to happen was his misfortune.'

It was almost as though, despite the innumerable earlier historical and artistic attestations, I was the only person to have loved Paris, because, to begin with, I saw no one else respond to this matter in the repugnant 'seventies.' But afterwards I learned that Louis Chevalier, the city's old historian, had published then, without too much being said about it, *The Assassination of Paris.* So we could count at least two righteous men in that city at the time. I did not want to see any more of this debasement of Paris. More generally, little importance should be granted the opinions of those who condemn something without having done whatever was necessary to destroy it or, failing that, who have at least shown themselves to be as alien to it as is still possible.

Chateaubriand pointed out, and rather accurately, all told: 'Of the modern French authors of my time, I am almost the only one whose life resembles his works.' In any case, I have most certainly lived as I have said one should; and this was perhaps even more unusual among the people of my day, who have all seemed to believe that they had to live only according to the instructions of those who direct current economic production and the power of communication with which it is armed. I have resided in Italy and Spain, principally in Florence and Seville – in Babylon, as it was called in the Golden Age – but also in other cities that were still living, and even in the countryside. I thus enjoyed a few pleasant years. Much later, when the flood of destruction, pollution, and falsification had conquered the whole surface of the planet, as well as pouring down nearly to its very depths, I could return to the ruins that remain of Paris, since by then nothing better was left elsewhere. No exile is possible in a unified world.

So what did I do during that time? I did not try too hard to avoid some dangerous encounters; it is even possible that I coolly sought some of them out.

In Italy I was admittedly not well thought of by everyone, but I had the good fortune to know the '*sfacciate donne fiorentine*' when I lived in Florence, in the Oltrarno district. There was that little Florentine who was so graceful. In the evenings she would cross the river to come to San Frediano. I fell in love very unexpectedly, perhaps because of a beautiful, bitter smile. And I said to her, in effect: 'Hold not thy peace, for I am a stranger with thee, and a sojourner. O spare me, that I may recover strength, before I go hence, and be no more.' Also at that time, Italy was once again losing its way: it was necessary to regain sufficient distance from its prisons, where those who stayed too long at the revels of Florence ended up.

The young Musset drew attention to himself long ago for his thoughtless question: 'In Barcelona, did you see / an Andalusian with sun-bronzed breasts?' Well, yes! I've had to say ever since 1980. I had my share – and perhaps a very large share – in the extravagances of Spain. But it was in another country that that irremediable princess, with her wild beauty and that voice, appeared. '*Mira como vengo yo,*' went the rather accurate words of the song she sang. That day we listened no more. I loved that Andalusian for a long time. How long? 'A time commensurate with our vain and paltry span,' as Pascal says.

I have even stayed in an inaccessible house surrounded by woods, far from any village, in an extremely barren, exhausted mountainous region, deep in a deserted Auvergne. I spent several winters there. Snow would fall for days on end. The wind piled it up in drifts. Barriers kept it off the road. Despite the surrounding walls, snow accumulated in the courtyard. Logs were piled high on the fire.

The house seemed to open directly onto the Milky Way. At night, the stars, so close, would shine brilliantly one moment, and the next be extinguished by the passing mist. And so too our conversations and revels, our meetings and tenacious passions.

It was a land of storms. They would approach silently at first, announced by the brief passage of a wind that slithered through the grass or by a series of sudden flashes on the horizon; then thunder and lightning would be unleashed, and we would be bombarded for a long while from every direction, as if in a fortress under siege. Just once, at night, I saw lightning strike near me outside: you could not even see where it had struck; the whole landscape was equally illuminated for one startling instant. Nothing in art has ever given me this impression of an irrevocable brilliance, except for the prose that Lautréamont employed in the programmatic exposition that he called *Poésies*. But nothing else: neither Mallarmé's blank page, nor Malevich's white square on a white background, nor even Goya's last pictures, where black takes over everything, as Saturn devours his children.

High winds, which at any moment could rise from one of three directions, shook the trees. The more dispersed trees on the heath to the north dipped and shook like ships surprised at anchor in an unprotected harbour. The compactly grouped trees that guarded the hillock in front of the house supported one another in their resistance, the first rank breaking the west wind's relentless assault. Farther off, the alignment of the woods laid out in squares, over the whole half-circle of the hills, evoked the troops ranged in a checkerboard pattern in certain eighteenth-century battle scenes. And those almost always vain charges sometimes made a breach, knocking down a rank. Masses of clouds traversed the sky at a run. A sudden change of wind could also quickly send them into retreat, with other clouds launched in their pursuit.

On calm mornings, there were all the birds of the dawn and the perfect chill of the air, and that dazzling shade of tender green that came over the trees, in the tremulous light of the sun rising before them.

The weeks went by imperceptibly. One day the morning air would announce the arrival of autumn. Another time, a great sweetness in the air, a sweetness you could taste, would declare itself, like a quick promise always kept, 'the first breath of spring.'

In regard to someone who has been, as essentially and continually as I, a man of streets and cities – one will thus appreciate the degree to which my preferences do not overly distort my judgments – it should be pointed out that the charm and harmony of these few seasons of grandiose isolation did not escape me. It was a pleasing and impressive solitude. But to tell the truth, I was not alone: I was with Alice.

In the midwinter nights of 1988, in the Square des Missions Étrangères, an owl would obstinately repeat his calls, fooled perhaps by the unseasonable weather. And this extraordinary series of encounters with the bird of Minerva, its atmosphere of surprise and indignation, did not in the least seem to constitute an allusion to the imprudent conduct or the various aberrations of my life. I have never understood where my life could have been different or how it ought to be justified.

V

'As a scholar and a man of learned education, and in that sense a gentleman, I may presume to class myself as an unworthy member of that indefinite body called gentlemen. Partly on the ground I have assigned, perhaps; partly because, from my having no visible calling or business ... I am so classed by my neighbours ...'

THOMAS DE QUINCEY,
Confessions of an English Opium Eater.

A COMBINATION of circumstances has marked almost everything I have done with a certain air of conspiracy. In this very era, many new professions have been created at great cost for the sole purpose of showing what beauty society had recently been able to achieve, and how soundly it reasoned in all its discourses and projects. Whereas I, without any salary, provided an example of entirely contrary schemes; this has inevitably been badly received. It has also led me to know, in several countries, people who were quite rightly considered lost. The police keep watch on them. That special kind of thought which can be considered the police form of knowledge expressed itself with reference to me in 1984, in the *Journal du Dimanche* of 18 March: 'For many police investigators, whether they belong to the crime squad, the DST, or the Renseignements généraux, the most serious trail leads to the entourage of Guy Debord ... The least that can be said is that, faithful to his legend, Guy Debord has hardly proved talkative.' Even earlier, in the *Nouvel Observateur* of 22 May 1972: 'The author of *The Society of the Spectacle* has always appeared as the discreet but indisputable head ... at the centre of the changing constellation of brilliant subversive conspirators of the Situationist International, a kind of cool chess player, rigorously leading ... the game whose every move he has foreseen. Surrounding himself with people of talent and good will, with his authority disguised. Then disbanding them with the same nonchalant virtuosity, manoeuvring his acolytes like naive pawns, clearing the board move after move, finally emerging as the sole master, while always dominating the game.'

My sort of mind leads me at first to be amazed at this, but it must be recognized that many of life's experiences only verify and illustrate the most conventional ideas, which one may have already encountered in numerous books but without believing them. Recalling what one has experienced oneself, one does not have to inquire into every detail of the observation never made or the surprising paradox. Thus I owe it to the truth

to note, as others have done, that the English
police seemed to me the most suspicious and the
most polite, the French police the most dangerously trained in historical interpretation, the
Italian police the most cynical, the Belgian police
the most rustic, the German police the most
arrogant; while it was the Spanish police who
proved themselves the least rational and the most
incompetent.

For an author who writes with a certain degree
of quality, and thus knows what it means to
speak, it is generally a sad ordeal when he has to
reread and consent to sign his own answers in a
statement for the *police judiciaire.* First, the text
as a whole is determined by the investigators'
questions, which are usually not recorded in the
text, and which do not innocently arise, as they
sometimes strive to appear, from the simple
logical necessities of a precise inquiry or for a
clear understanding. The answers that one has
been able to formulate are in fact hardly better
than their summary, which is dictated by the
highest-ranking officer and rewritten with a considerable degree of obvious awkwardness and
vagueness. If, naturally – but many innocents are
unaware of this – it is imperative to insist on the
precise correction of every detail in which the
thought that one expressed has been rendered with

a deplorable unfaithfulness, one must quickly give up any notion of having everything transcribed in the proper and satisfactory form that one used spontaneously, for then one would be led to double the number of those already tiresome hours, which would rid the greatest purist of his desire for such purity. So then, I here declare that my answers to the police should not be published later in my collected works, because of scruples about the form, and even though I had no hesitation in signing my name to their veracious content.

Having certainly, thanks to one of the rare positive features of my early education, acquired a sense of discretion, I have sometimes known the necessity of demonstrating a discretion still more pronounced. A number of useful habits have thus become like second nature to me; this I say while conceding nothing to malevolent persons who might be capable of claiming that such habits could in no way be distinguished from my very nature. No matter what the subject, I trained myself to be even less interesting whenever I saw greater chances of being overheard. In some cases, I also made appointments or gave my opinions through letters personally addressed to friends and modestly signed with little-known names that have figured in the entourage of certain famous poets: Colin Decayeux or Guido Cavalcanti, for example. But it is quite obvious that I have never stooped to publishing anything whatsoever under a pseudonym, despite what some hack libellers sometimes insinuated in the press, with an extraordinary aplomb, though prudently confining themselves to the most abstract generalities.

It is permitted, but not desirable, to wonder where such a predilection to challenging all authorities could positively lead. 'We never seek things for themselves but for the search'; certainty on this subject is long established. 'One prefers the hunt to the catch ...'

Our era of technicians makes abundant use of the nominalized adjective 'professional'; it seems to believe that therein lies some kind of guarantee. Of course, if one contemplates not my emoluments but only my abilities, no one can doubt that I have been a very good professional. But in what domain? Such will have been my mystery, in the eyes of a blameworthy world.

Messrs Blin, Chavanne, and Drago, who together published a *Traité du Droit de la Presse* [Treatise on Press Law] in 1969, concluded the chapter concerning the 'Danger of apologias' with an authority and experience that felicitously lead me to believe that they should be accorded a great deal of confidence: 'To vindicate a criminal act, to present it as glorious, praiseworthy, or lawful, can have considerable persuasive power. Weak-willed individuals who read such apologias will not only feel absolved in advance if they commit those acts, but will even see in their commission the opportunity of becoming important people. The knowledge of criminal psychology shows the danger of apologias.'

VI

'And when I think that these people march side by side, on
a long, hard journey, in order to arrive together at the same
place, where they will run a thousand dangers to achieve
a great and noble goal, these reflections give this picture
a meaning that profoundly moves me.'

CARL VON CLAUSEWITZ, Letter of 18 September 1806.

I HAVE been very interested in war, in the theorists of strategy but also in recollections of battles or the many other conflicts history mentions – surface eddies on the river of time. I am not unaware that war is the domain of danger and disappointment, perhaps even more so than the other sides of life. This consideration has not, however, diminished the attraction that I have felt for that particular side.

And so I have studied the logic of war. Moreover, I succeeded, a long time ago, in presenting the basics of its movements on a rather simple board game: the forces in contention as well as the contradictory necessities imposed on the operations of each of the two parties. I have played this game and, in the often difficult conduct of my life, I have drawn a few lessons from it – I also set myself rules of the game for this life, and I have followed them. The surprises of this kriegspiel seem inexhaustible; and I fear that this may well be the only one of my works that anyone will dare acknowledge as having some value. As to whether I have made good use of such lessons, I will leave it to others to decide.

It must be acknowledged that those amongst us who have been able to perform wonders with writing have often shown less evidence of expertise in the command of war. The trials and tribulations met with on this terrain are now innumerable. During the retreat from Prague, Captain de Vauvenargues marched along with troops who were pushed hard in the one direction still open. 'Hunger and disorder tramp in their fugitive tracks; night shrouds their steps and death stalks them in silence ... Fires lit on the ice illuminate their last moments; the earth is their fearsome bed.' And Gondi was distressed to see the regiment that he had just raised about-face quickly on the Pont d'Antony, and to hear this rout referred to as the 'First Corinthians.' And Charles d'Orléans was in the vanguard of the ill-fated attack at Agincourt, which was riddled with arrows along its course and broken at its end, where one could see 'all the gentle and chivalrous nobles of France, who were at least ten to one against the English, be thus defeated.' He was to remain captive in England for twenty-five years, little appreciating on his return the manners of another generation ('The world is bored with me / and just so I with it'). And Thucydides had the misfortune to arrive with the fleet he commanded a few hours too late to prevent the fall of Amphipolis; he could only ward off one of the many consequences of the disaster by landing his infantry at Eion, which saved that town. Lieutenant von Clausewitz himself, with the fine army marching on Jena, was far from expecting what they would find there.

But all the same, at the Battle of Neerwinden in Royal-Roussillon, Captain de Saint-Simon gallantly took part in the five charges by the cavalry, which as a fixed target had already been exposed to the fire of enemy cannon whose balls swept away whole files, while the ranks of 'the insolent nation' kept re-forming. And Stendhal, second lieutenant in the Sixth Dragoons in Italy, captured an Austrian battery. As the Battle of Lepanto raged on the sea, Cervantes, at the head of twelve men, was unshakeable in holding the last redoubt of his galley when the Turks tried to board it. Archilochus was said to be a professional soldier. And Dante, when the Florentine cavalry charged at Campaldino, killed his man there, and still took pleasure in evoking it in Canto V of the *Purgatorio*: 'And I to him: "What violence or what chance / Led thee astray so far from Campaldino / That never has thy sepulture been known?"'

History is affecting. If the best authors, taking part in its struggles, have proved at times less excellent in this regard than in their writings, history, on the other hand, has never failed to find people who had the instinct for the happy turn of phrase to communicate its passions to us. 'The Vendée no longer exists,' General Westermann wrote to the Convention in December 1793, after his victory at Savenay. 'It died under our sabres along with its women and children. I have just buried it in the marshes and woods of Savenay. I have crushed the children under the hooves of our horses, massacred the women – those at least will not give birth to any more brigands. I have not even one prisoner to reproach myself for. I have exterminated everyone ... We take no prisoners, for we would have to give them the bread of liberty, and pity is not revolutionary.' A few months later, Westermann was to be executed with the Dantonists, who were branded with the name 'the Indulgents.' Shortly before the insurrection of 10 August 1792, an officer of the Swiss Guards, the last remaining defenders of the monarch's person, wrote a letter that sincerely expressed the sentiments of his comrades: 'All of us said that if any harm came to the king, and there were not at least six hundred red coats lying at the foot of the king's stairway, we would be dishonoured.' A little more than six hundred guards were indeed killed when the same Westermann, who had first tried to neutralize the soldiers by advancing alone among them on the king's stairway and speaking to them in German, realized there was nothing for it but to launch the attack.

In the Vendée, still fighting on, a 'Song to Rally the Chouans in the Event of a Rout' declared just as stubbornly: 'We have only one life to live, / we owe it to honour. / That's the flag we must follow…' During the Mexican Revolution, Francisco Villa's partisans sang: 'Of that famous Division of the North, / now only a few of us are left, / still crossing the mountains, / finding someone to fight wherever we go.' And the American volunteers of the Lincoln Brigade sang in 1937: 'There's a valley in Spain called Jarama / It's a place that we all know so well, / For 'tis there that we wasted our manhood / And most of our old age as well.' A song of the Germans in the Foreign Legion expressed a more detached melancholy: 'Where in the world are you going,

Anne-Marie? / I'm going to town where the soldiers are.' Montaigne had his quotations; I have mine. Soldiers are marked by a past, not by a future. That is why their songs can touch us.

In *Villes*, Pierre Mac Orlan recalled the attack on Bouchavesne, which was entrusted to young ruffians serving in the French army, assigned by law to the African light-infantry battalions: 'On the road to Bapaume, not far from Bouchavesne and Rancourt, where the "Joyeux" redeemed their sins in a few hours, climbing up a mound, the mound of the Berlingots Woods, one caught sight of Picardy and its torn dress.' On the opposing slopes of this sentence, with its skilful awkwardness, which this mound overhangs, one recognizes memory and its superimposed meanings.

Herodotus reports that at the pass of Thermopylae, where the troops led by Leonidas were annihilated at the end of their useful holding action, next to the inscriptions that evoke the hopeless combat of 'Four thousand men from the Peloponnesus' and the Three Hundred who had it said in Sparta that they lie there, 'obedient to their orders,' the seer Megistias is honoured with a special epitaph: 'A seer, he knew that death was near – but he refused to leave the Spartan leader.' One does not have to be a seer to know that there is no position so good that it cannot be outflanked by much superior forces, or even be overwhelmed by a frontal attack. But it is good to be indifferent to this sort of knowledge, in some cases. The world of war at least presents the advantage of not leaving room for the silly chatter of optimism. It is common knowledge that in the end everyone is going to die. No matter how fine one's defence may be in everything else, as Pascal more or less put it, 'the last act is bloody.'

What discovery could still be expected in this domain? The telegram sent by the King of Prussia to Queen Augusta, on the eve of the Battle of Saint-Privat, sums up most wars: 'The troops performed prodigies of valour against an equally brave enemy.' The brief text of the order, briskly relayed by an officer, which sent the Light Brigade to its death on 25 October 1854 at Balaclava, is well known: 'Lord Raglan wishes the cavalry to advance rapidly to the front – follow the enemy and try to prevent the enemy carrying away the guns ...' It is true that the wording is a little imprecise; but no matter what anyone has said, it is no more obscure or erroneous than a multitude of plans and orders that have directed historic undertakings to their uncertain ends or inevitably dire outcomes. It is amusing to see what superior airs journalistic and academic thinkers put on when it comes to giving their opinions on the plans for military operations now over. Since the result is known, they need at least one victory in the field to make them refrain from derision and limit themselves to observations on the excessive price in blood and the relative limits of the success achieved, compared to others that, according to them, would have been possible on that day if one had gone about it more intelligently. These same thinkers have always listened with a great deal of respect to the worst visionaries of technology and all the dreamers of the economy, without even thinking of examining the results.

Masséna was fifty-seven years old when he said that command wears one out, as he spoke before his staff when he had been charged with conducting the conquest of Portugal: 'You don't live twice in our profession, no more so than on this earth.' Time does not wait. One does not defend Genoa twice; no one has twice roused Paris to revolt. Xerxes, as his great army was crossing the Hellespont, perhaps formulated in just one sentence the first axiom at the base of all strategic thought, when he explained his tears by saying: 'It came into my mind how pitifully short human life is – for of all these thousands of men not one will be alive in a hundred years' time.'

VII

'But if these Memoirs ever see the light, I have no doubt that they will incite a prodigious revolt ... and as in the times in which I wrote, especially most recently, everything tended towards decadence, confusion, chaos, which have only grown in the meantime, and since these Memoirs exude nothing but order, rule, truth, fixed principles, and expose everything that is to the contrary, which increasingly reigns with the most ignorant, albeit the highest possible authority, then the furore against this truthful mirror ought to be widespread.'

SAINT-SIMON, *Memoirs.*

A DESCRIPTION in *The Rural Life of England,*
which Howitt published in 1840, exhibited a no
doubt excessively generalized satisfaction when
it was able to conclude, 'Let every man who has
a sufficiency for the enjoyment of life, thank
heaven most fervently that he lives in this country
and age.' In contrast, there is little chance of our
age over-emphasizing, with regard to the life that
is lived now, the general disgust and the beginnings of fright that are felt in so many domains.
They are felt but never expressed before bloody
revolts. The reasons for this are simple. The
pleasures of existence have recently been redefined in an authoritarian way – first in their
priorities and then in their entire substance. And
the authorities who redefined them could just as
well decide at any moment, untroubled by any

other consideration, which modification might be most lucratively introduced into the techniques of their manufacture, entirely liberated from any need to please. For the first time, the same people are the masters of everything that is done and of everything that is said about what is done. And so Madness 'hath builded her house in the high places of the city.'

The only thing proposed to people who did not enjoy such indisputable and universal competence was to submit, without adding the least critical remark, on this question of their sense of the pleasures of existence – just as they had already elected representatives of their submission everywhere else. And they have shown, in letting themselves be relieved of these trivialities, which they have been told are unworthy of their attention, the same affability they had already demonstrated by watching, from a greater distance, life's few remaining glories slip away. When 'to be absolutely modern' has become a special law decreed by some tyrant, what the honest slave fears more than anything is that he might be suspected of being behind the times.

Men more knowledgeable than I have explained very well the origin of what has come to pass: 'Exchange value could arise only as a representative of use value, but the victory it eventually won with its own weapons created the conditions for its own autonomous power. By mobilizing all human use value and monopolizing its fulfilment, exchange value ultimately succeeded in *controlling use*. Usefulness has come to be seen purely in terms of exchange value, and is now completely at its mercy. Starting out like a condottiere in the service of use value, exchange value has ended up waging the war for its own sake.'

'Le monde n'est qu'abusion' – 'The world is naught but deception,' as Villon summed it up in one octosyllable. (It is an octosyllable, even though nowadays a college graduate would probably be capable of recognizing only six syllables in this line.) The general decadence is a means in the service of the empire of servitude, and it is only as this means that it is permitted to be called progress.

One should know that servitude henceforth truly wants to be loved for its own sake and no longer because it might bring some extrinsic advantage. Previously, it could pass for a protection, but it no longer protects anything. Nowadays servitude does not try to justify itself by claiming to have preserved, anywhere at all, any charm except the pleasure of experiencing it.

I will speak later of how certain phases of another, not very well known war unfolded:

between the general tendency of social domination in this era and what managed, despite everything, to come and disrupt it, as we know.

Although I am a remarkable example of what this era did not want, knowing what it has wanted seems to me perhaps not enough to establish my excellence. Swift says, with a great deal of truthfulness, in the first book of his *History of the Four Last Years of the Queen*: 'Neither shall I mingle Panegyrick or Satire with an History intended to inform Posterity, as well as to instruct those of the present Age, who may be Ignorant or Misled; Since Facts, truly related, are the best Applauses, or most lasting Reproaches.' No one knew better than Shakespeare how life passes. He finds that 'we are such stuff as dreams are made on.' Calderón came to the same conclusion. I am at least assured, by the foregoing, of having succeeded in conveying the elements that will suffice to make abundantly clear, so that no sort of mystery or illusion might remain, all that I am.

Here the author closes his true history: forgive him his faults.

Panegyric

VOLUME 2

GUY DEBORD

Translated by John McHale

I would like to thank Alice Debord,
Eamon Butterfield, James Brook, Donald
Nicholson-Smith, and Jonathon Green for
their help with this translation. Thanks too go
to Jane Hindle, Tim Clark, Andrea Stimpson,
and Andrea Woodman at Verso.

John McHale
London, 2004.

'I have followed an unusual plan, having devised a new method of writing history and chosen a path that will surprise the reader – a course and a system that are entirely my own.'

IBN KHALDÛN, *The Muqaddimah: An Introduction to History.*

AUTHOR'S NOTE

OF ALL the truths which go to make up this volume
of *Panegyric*, it will be acknowledged that the
most profound resides in the very manner of
assembling and presenting them together. There
scarcely remains anything more to do then but
illustrate and comment on the essential, which is
already to be found summed up so precisely in the
first volume.

The second volume contains a set of icono-
graphical evidence. The reigning deceptions of the
time are on the point of making us forget that
the truth may also be found in images. An image
that has not been deliberately separated from
its meaning adds great precision and certainty
to knowledge. Until very recently, no one has
ever doubted it. I intend, however, to provide a
reminder of it now. An authentic illustration sheds

light on true discourse, like a subordinate clause which is neither incompatible nor pleonastic.

People will at last be able to see what I looked like at various ages of my life, the kinds of faces that have always surrounded me, and what kind of places I have lived in. All these things taken together and considered will serve to round off their final opinion. For example, my contribution – one which constitutes a rather singular historical monument – to extremist art in this century shall be displayed herein in its entirety: the mark of its excellence resides in the little there is.

This coherent documentation will be supplemented by various data, for example, graphological, which ought to be looked on as superfluous. Yet in like manner, those who prefer to believe in the existence of various simpler and more direct methods of knowledge than the science of history, or who at least trust to one or the other as a means of verification, will have the displeasure of being sure that they can find nothing to hold against me.

The most notable dates of my works, whose unity may thus be fully appreciated, are listed at the end of the present volume. In the third volume, several details which still remain obscure will receive explanation.*

* The third volume, along with the succeeding ones still at manuscript stage, were burned during the night of 30 November 1994, in accordance with Guy Debord's wishes. – *Publisher*.

1

'Our only public activities ... were meant to be completely
unacceptable: at first, primarily due to their form; later,
as they acquired depth, primarily due to their content.'

1951

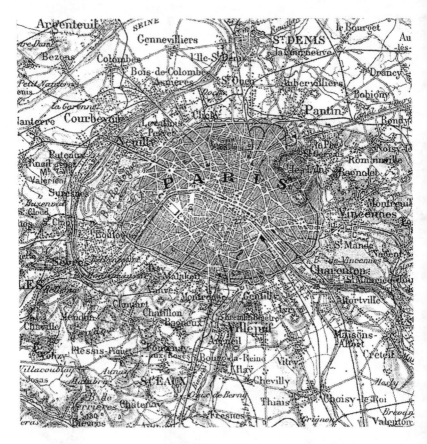

THE CITY OF PARIS

'It is true that the idea we have fashioned for ourselves of
earlier civilizations has become more dispassionate since
... we have begun to look as well as to read. The plastic
arts do not lament.'

HUIZINGA, *The Autumn of the Middle Ages.*

A TWENTY-FOUR-MINUTE SEQUENCE OF BLACK SCREEN
FROM THE FILM *HOWLS FOR SADE* (1952)

'Before speaking, he fired a few pistol shots into the air
and then proceeded, sometimes laughing, sometimes in
deadly earnest, to inveigh against art and life in the most
demented terms imaginable.'

Paris-Midi (6 July 1914);
included in Arthur Cravan's *Oeuvres*.

le public se sentait atteint dans sa dignité et criait au fou

on entendait les cris aigus des bonnes femmes et
les injures des hommes. Les salauds, ordures,
fumiers, assassins, bouchers, résonnaient

CINE-CLUB : Vous assistez à la projection du premier film raté

Les arts futurs seront des bouleverse

RUE DE SEINE: INSCRIPTION ON A WALL (1953)

'This prejudiced the World so much at first, that several of
my Friends had the Assurance to ask me, Whether I were
in jest? To which I only answered coldly, *That the Event
will show*.'

SWIFT, *Predictions for the Year 1708.*

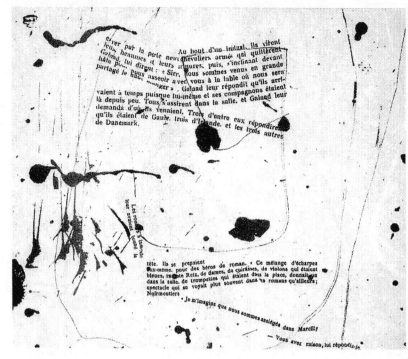

1959: *MÉMOIRES* (DETAIL)

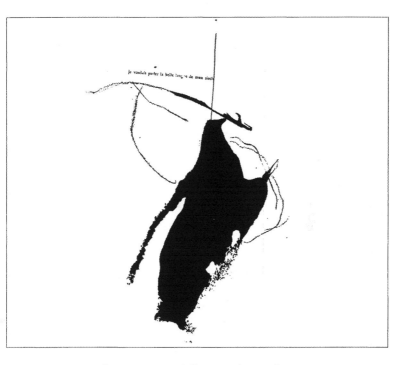

LAST PAGE OF *MÉMOIRES* (DETAIL)

2

'All revolutions run into history, yet history is not full;
unto the place from whence the rivers of revolution come,
thither they return again.'

1953

THE BANKS OF THE SEINE

'A peculiarity that those who write history will be unaware of, or else consider not worth mentioning. Nevertheless, it is this very peculiarity that reveals whether we merit esteem or blame.'

FRANÇOISE DE MOTTEVILLE, *Mémoires*.

'We are too unobservant or too self-centred to fathom one another. Anyone who has seen masks at a ball, dancing amicably together, and holding hands without recognizing one another, only to part a moment later, and neither to meet again nor miss one another, can form a conception of the world at large.'

VAUVENARGUES, *Reflections and Maxims.*

IVAN CHTCHEGLOV

'We are merely at the beginning of the art of writing ...
Each life has a theme, a title, a publisher, a preface, an
introduction, a text, notes, etc. – or could have them.'

NOVALIS, *Fragments.*

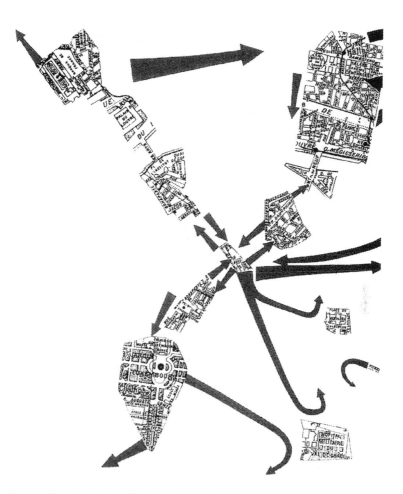

THE NAKED CITY

'If Montpipeau's your next stop,
Or Ruel, watch you don't take the drop.
For playing these spots fast and loose
Colin de Cayeux got the topman's noose.'

VILLON, 'A Sterling Lesson for Lost Children.'

1, Impasse de Clairvaux

'All this is gone forever – events, men, everything slips away, like the ceaseless waves of the Yangtze that vanish into the sea.'

LI PO, 'At Nanking.'

3

'A combination of circumstances has marked almost everything I have done with a certain air of conspiracy.'

1958

Cosio d'Arroscia (Ligurian Alps)

'And while we drink, let us also drink to our own glory, that our grandsons and, after them, the sons of our grandsons might one day say that once there lived men who did not disgrace their comradeship and did not betray their own friends.'

GOGOL, *Taras Bulba.*

ASGER JORN

32, RUE DE LA MONTAGNE-SAINTE-GENEVIÈVE

'This work will demonstrate the greatness of this prince of
whom I tell you, and also your own understanding.'

COMMYNES, *Mémoires.*

'DIRECTIVE NO. 2' (1963)

'Of our philosopher Timon gives a sketch in these words: "In their midst uprose shrill, cuckoo-like, a mob-reviler, riddling Heraclitus." Theophrastus puts it down to melancholy that some parts of his work are half-finished, while other parts make a strange medley ... Such great fame did his book win that a sect was founded and called the Heracliteans, after him.'

DIOGENES LAERTIUS,
Lives, Opinions, and Sayings of Eminent Philosophers.

OTHER ILLUSTRATED PREDICTIONS

[Translations of comic strips:]

[1]

'It is thus the very evolution of class society into
the spectacular organization of non-life that obliges
the revolutionary project to become *visibly* what it
always was *in essence.*'

[2]

'Everything points to a crisis in this organization! …
Some elements are being purged! …'

[3]

'I'm sorry, Wanter, but I want nothing to do
with this type of policy. I'm submitting my
resignation to you.'

'You are free to pull out, Wodran, as are
those who share your scruples.'

Four council members left the assembly room …
the meeting was adjourned, but President Wanter
showed no willingness to change his policy.

Down a dark alley in Chinatown,
not far from the docks …

[2nd cartoon]
'Hello George! The owl of Minerva?…'

'… takes flight at dusk! They're in the back.'

'My assumption was that the surest way of arriving at useful discoveries was to stand aloof in all ways from the paths followed by the inexact sciences, none of which has made any discovery remotely useful to the social body, and which, despite the immense progress of industry, have not even managed to prevent poverty. My task, as I saw it, was thus to maintain a constant oppositional stance with regard to that body of knowledge. Looking at the huge number of writers involved, I assumed that any subject that they had dealt with must be thoroughly exhausted, and I decided to tackle only problems which none of them had attempted to investigate.'

FOURIER, *The Theory of the Four Movements.*

— 1 —

Toute la vie des sociétés dans lesquelles règnent les conditions modernes de production s'annonce comme une immense accumulation de spectacles. Tout ce qui était directement vécu s'en est éloigné dans une représentation.

— 2 —

Les images qui se sont détachées de chaque aspect de la vie fusionnent dans un cours commun, où l'unité de cette vie ne peut plus être rétablie. La spécialisation des images du monde se retrouve, accomplie, dans le monde de l'image autonomisé, où le mensonger s'est menti à lui-même. Le spectacle, comme inversion concrète de la vie, est le mouvement autonome du non-vivant.

— 3 —

Le spectacle se présente à la fois comme la société même, comme une partie de la société, et comme instrument d'unification. En tant que partie de la société, il est expressément le secteur qui concentre tout regard et toute conscience. Du fait même que ce secteur est séparé, il est le lieu du regard abusé et de la fausse conscience; et l'unification qu'il accomplit n'est rien d'autre qu'un langage officiel de la séparation généralisée.

— 4 —

Le spectacle n'est pas un ensemble d'images, mais un rapport social entre des personnes, médiatisé par des images.

MANUSCRIPT OF *THE SOCIETY OF THE SPECTACLE* (1967)

121

'On death ground, look for the chance to fight. By death ground I mean those places where you cannot count on a single resource, where you are slowly worn down by inclement weather, where your supplies are gradually used up without any hope of obtaining fresh ones; where disease, already starting to make inroads into the army, looks set to decimate it before long. In circumstances such as these, make haste to give some form of battle.'

SUN TZU, *The Art of War.*

A BAS
LA SOCIÉTÉ SPECTACULAIRE-MARCHANDE

CONSEIL POUR LE MAINTIEN DES OCCUPATIONS

'DOWN WITH SPECTACLE-COMMODITY SOCIETY'
COUNCIL FOR MAINTAINING THE OCCUPATIONS

POSTERITY OF THE 'DIRECTIVES' IN THE EPIGRAPHY OF 1968

'Humanity will only be happy the day the last bureaucrat
is hanged with the guts of the last capitalist.'
[Translation of graffito on painting]

'Cobblestones turn me on.' [Graffito on opposite page]

ALICE BECKER-HO

[Opposite page]
'END OF THE UNIVERSITY'
COUNCIL FOR MAINTAINING THE OCCUPATIONS

CONSEIL POUR LE MAINTIEN DES OCCUPATIONS

'So ended this winter, and the eighteenth year of the war written by Thucydides.'

THUCYDIDES, *History of the Peloponnesian War.*

4

'I have known the world quite well, then, its history and geography, its landscapes and those who populated them.'

1968

RESIDING IN ITALY AND SPAIN

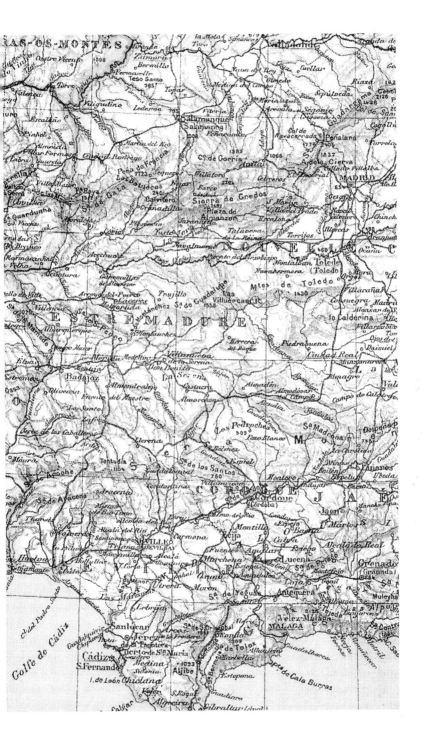

CADIZ

Profondeurs
de 0 à 10ᵐ / plus de 10ᵐ

S.Sebastian

CADIZ

Puntales

F.ᵗ S.Fernando

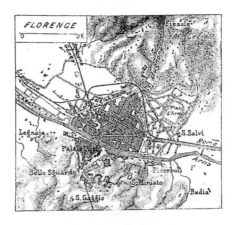

FLORENCE

Fiesole

Mᵗᵉ Ceceri

Legnaja

Piau
d'Arno

S.Salvi

Roma

Palais Pitti

Arno

Bello Sguardo

Ricorboli

S.Miniato

Budia

S.Gaggio

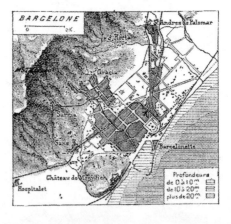

BARCELONE

S.Andres de Palomar

S.Horta

Gracia

Sarria

Sans

Château de Monjuich

Barcelonetta

Hospitalet

Profondeurs
de 0 à 10ᵐ
de 10 à 20ᵐ
plus de 20ᵐ

THE OLTRARNO IN 1972

'The French are by nature fond of the goods of others, and at the same time extremely prodigal as much with their own as with those of others.'

MACHIAVELLI, *Report on Affairs in France.*

28, Via delle Caldaie

PIEVE IN THE CHIANTI HILLS

CHAMPOT

'As little as *we* can be declared clear of every coercion in
the world, so little can our writing be withdrawn from it.
But as free as we are, so free can we make it too.'

MAX STIRNER, *The Ego and Its Own.*

"'If I were to show her to you," replied Don Quixote, "what merit would there be in you confessing so obvious a truth? The essence of the matter is that you must believe, confess, affirm, swear and maintain it without seeing her.

If you will not, ... Here I stand and await you, confident in the right which I have on my side.'"

CERVANTES, *Don Quixote*.

5

'I have been very interested in war ... in presenting the basics of its movements on a rather simple board game: the forces in contention as well as the contradictory necessities imposed on the operations of each of the two parties.'

1977

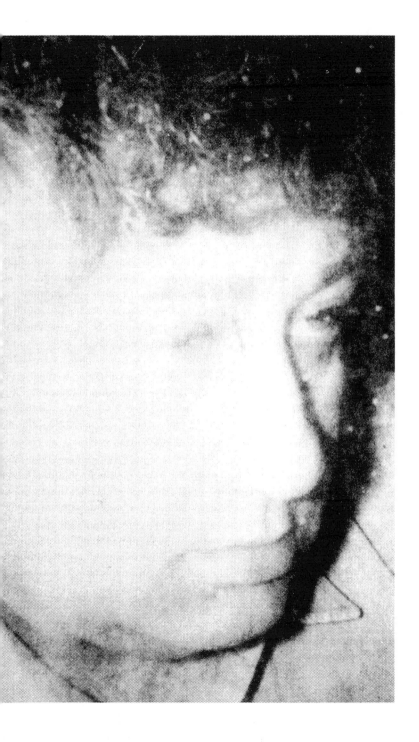

'I will say above all that in order to be strong at the points you attack, it is almost indispensable to be weak on those you are defending, and that whenever a detachment is beaten the consequences are far less dire when it is few in number than when it is numerically strong; that moreover the weaker it is, the less it is exposed to defeat, because its leader redoubles his vigilance and precautionary measures in order to avoid situations in which he could well find himself dangerously engaged.'

GOUVION SAINT-CYR, *Mémoires.*

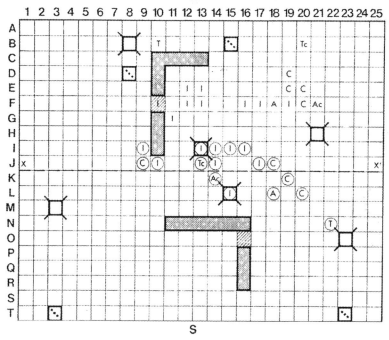

Diagram of the thirtieth stage
of a conflict on the kriegspiel

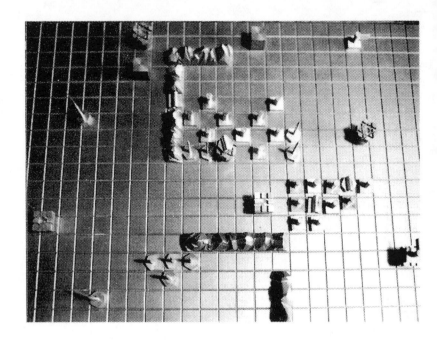

'We fear much more from an enemy than he can really carry out, and although our experience may be substantial, we cannot help but dread things which we know full well we would never do, were we in his place; but because great harm would result were an enemy in fact to do more than we anticipated, we prefer to remedy even what we think he cannot do.'

TURENNE, *Mémoires.*

THE LIGHT BRIGADE IN THE FILM
IN GIRUM IMUS NOCTE ET CONSUMIMUR IGNI

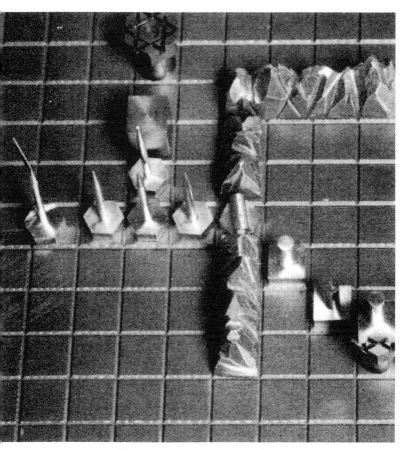

THE KRIEGSPIEL (DETAIL)

'If the progress made lately by the art of war has sufficiently demonstrated that a mountainous region cannot be defended by means of a system of cordons and of great fortified lines, it is equally true to say that noticeably better results would not be obtained by occupying strong transversal and longitudinal positions on the floors of valleys, without at the same time holding the heights that dominate them.'

LIEUTENANT-COLONEL RACCHIA,
Précis analytique de l'art de la guerre.

6

'In the midwinter nights of 1988, in the Square des Missions Étrangères, an owl would obstinately repeat his calls, fooled perhaps by the unseasonable weather.'

1984

The Square des Missions Étrangères

Ces *Commentaires* sont assurés d'être promptement connus de cinquante ou soixante personnes; autant dire beaucoup dans les jours que nous vivons, et quand on traite de questions si graves. Mais aussi c'est parce que j'ai, dans certains milieux, la réputation d'être un connaisseur. Il faut également considérer que, de cette élite qui va s'y intéresser, la moitié, ou un nombre qui s'en approche de très près, est composée de gens qui s'emploient à maintenir le système de domination spectaculaire, et l'autre moitié de gens qui s'obstineront à faire tout le contraire. Ayant ainsi à tenir compte de lecteurs très attentifs et diversement influents, je ne peux évidemment parler en toute liberté. Je dois surtout prendre garde à ne pas trop instruire n'importe qui.

Le malheur des temps m'obligera donc à écrire, encore une fois, d'une façon nouvelle. Certains

FIRST PAGE OF THE 1988 *COMMENTS*

'But because my sole intention here has been to make remarks that are entirely distinct from one another, with the comprehension of a particular one in no way depending upon an understanding of the ones placed either before or after it, connecting them would only have caused difficulties, and I might very well have found myself going out of my way to make my work less agreeable and less useful to the reader. For there is no doubt that this continual diversity of subject matter creates the spirit anew and renders it more capable of carrying out what is proposed to it, especially when, as is the case here, brevity has been added to the general aspect, and one has been assured that every remark will make its effect felt.'

VAUGELAS, *Remarques sur la langue française.*

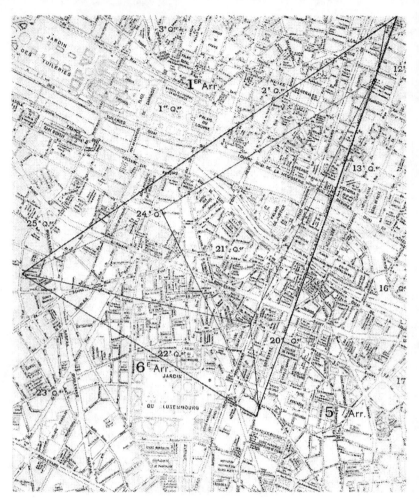

RESIDING IN PARIS

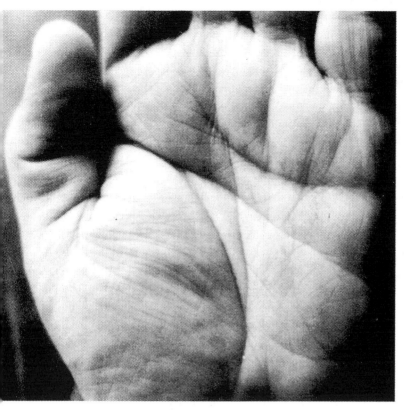

THE AUTHOR'S HAND

'Men at some time are masters of their fates:
The fault, dear Brutus, is not in our stars,
But in ourselves, that we are underlings.'

SHAKESPEARE, *Julius Caesar.*

CONCLUSIONS SEQUENCE IN THE FILM
THE SOCIETY OF THE SPECTACLE

[Caption:]
'I can't help it,' said the scorpion. 'It's my character.'

GUY DEBORD

PANÉGYRIQUE

TOME PREMIER

'But I must here, once and for all, inform you, that all this
will be more exactly delineated and explained in a map, now
in the hands of the engraver, which, with many other pieces
and developments to this work, will be added to the end of
the twentieth volume, – not to swell the work, – I detest
the thought of such a thing; – but by way of commentary,
scholium, illustration, and key to such passages, incidents,
or innuendoes as shall be thought to be either of private
interpretation, or of dark or doubtful meaning after my life
and my opinions shall have been read over, (now don't forget
the meaning of the word) by all the *world* ...'

STERNE, *The Life and Opinions of Tristram Shandy.*

CHRONOLOGICAL OUTLINE

1931. Birth in Paris, on 28 December, at nightfall.

1952. Full-length film containing no images, *Howls for Sade*.

1953. Inscription on a wall along Rue de Seine.

1954. First issue of the bulletin *Potlatch*.

1957. The Situationist International is founded at the Cosio d'Arroscia Conference.

1958. First issue of the journal *Internationale Situationniste*.

1959. *Mémoires* composed solely of diverted sentences [*phrases détournées*].

1963. Five 'directives' inscribed on canvases.

1967. *The Society of the Spectacle*.

1968. For two days a Situationist committee usurps the Sorbonne and, within its walls, refutes seven centuries of stupidity.

1972. Autodissolution of the Situationist International.

1973. *The Society of the Spectacle* reiterated in the form of a full-length film.

1978. Full-length film, *In girum imus nocte et consumimur igni*.

1984. A potlatch of destruction targets this entire cinematic oeuvre.

1988. *Comments on the Society of the Spectacle*.

1989. First volume of *Panegyric*.

(Continuation)*

1991. Guy Debord breaks off relations with the heirs
        to Éditions Gérard Lebovici and demands that
        all remaining copies of his books be pulped.

1992. With Jean-Jacques Pauvert acting as
        go-between, Éditions Gallimard republish
        seven titles by Guy Debord.

1993. *Cette mauvaise réputation ...* [This Bad
        Reputation ...].

1994. On 30 November, Guy Debord carries out
        one last potlatch: *the admirable thing about
        his death is that it cannot pass for accidental*,
        being by his own hand.

1995. On 9 January, *Guy Debord, son art et son
        temps* [Guy Debord: His Art and His Times]
        is screened on Canal Plus TV. A letter dated
        14 November had authorized the director of
        the channel to schedule a 'Guy Debord night
        for some time in January 1995, in a slot most
        convenient to you.' Guy Debord, true to his
        word, was not around to see it.

---

* Before the publication of *Panegyric, Volume 2*, this brief summary ended at
this point. We herewith furnish the remainder. – *Publisher*.

On the difficulties of translating *Panégyrique*

I

THE TRANSLATION of the first volume of *Panégyrique* presents numerous difficulties even if it is entrusted to a highly competent person; failing this, it is impossible. There is thus no way it should even be undertaken in the conditions of woeful deficiency that for several years now have sadly dominated the whole practice of translation in European publishing. Anyone who refuses to grasp the fact that this book contains many traps and multiple, deliberately intended meanings, or who has not managed to find somebody possessing the requisite qualifications and skills not to get hopelessly lost in its pages, should immediately give up all ambition of publishing it in a foreign language, thereby leaving the way clear for other, more competent publishers to carry out the task in the future.

It must first of all be borne in mind that, beneath the classical French – for which one has to have a feeling from the outset, and for which the translator needs to be able to give a foreign-language equivalent – there lies hidden an especially modern use of this 'classical language'; an innovation therefore as unusual as it is shocking. A translation must render the whole, and do so faithfully.

The greatest difficulty, however, is this: this book naturally contains a fair amount of information that must be rendered accurately in translation. But in the final analysis, the question is not one of information. For the most part, its information resides in the very manner in which it is expressed.

Each time – and there are frequent instances of this – that a word or sentence presents two possible meanings, *both of them* must be recognized and retained, for the sentence must be understood as wholly veracious with regard to both meanings. This also implies that the sole truth running through the entire text is the sum total of the possible meanings to be found therein.

To give a very general example of this effect, all the epigraphs to the chapters must first be understood, of course, as ironically levelled against the author. But the reader should also be aware of the fact that he is not apprehending merely irony here: in the final analysis, should they be perceived as truly ironic? The doubt surrounding this question should remain intact.

Different types of vocabulary (military, legal) are used conventionally according to the particular subjects touched upon, at the same time that the tones of quotations from very diverse epochs are blended into the text. The translator should not lack the ability, nor for that matter be surprised, to make out a word of familiar or even slang provenance, on the odd few occasions when these occur in the author's language. It will have been used deliberately, like salt, precisely to bring out the flavour of the others. Likewise, sometimes the irony is closely interwoven with the lyrical tone, without taking anything away from its positive gravity.

In any case, it is impossible at the present time to arrive at any proper conclusion about what the full and definitive meaning of this work will be: this remains wholly in abeyance, since it is only the first volume. The end of the book is projected outside itself.

This continual *shift* of meaning, which is more or less evident in every single sentence, is present too in the general movement of the entire book. Thus the question of language is dealt with through strategy (chapter I); the passions of love through criminality (chapter II); the passing of time through alcoholism (chapter III); the attraction to places through their destruction (chapter IV); the fondness for subversion through the police backlash that it continually incurs (chapter V); growing old through the sphere of war (chapter VI); decay through economic development (chapter VII).

A case in point may be quoted from page 26 in the form of this sentence: 'Somewhere between Rue du Four and Rue de Buci, where our youth was

173

so completely lost, as a few glasses were drunk, one could feel certain that we would never do anything better.' What exactly does this sentence mean? It means everything one could possibly read into it. In contempt of the good classical rule, it ought to be possible to join the apposition: 'as a few glasses were drunk' – in this case as a euphemism – onto the preceding phrase; but it ought *also* to be joined onto the phrase that comes after it, where it would act as a precise and instantaneous observation. But what is more, the subject represented by 'one' can be understood as being both an outside observer (and, in this case, an utterly disapproving one), and the subjective opinion held by this youth (giving vent, in this instance, to a satisfaction that may be deemed philosophically or cynically lucid). Everything is true, nothing must be excised.

II

Considering the complexity of this book, a publisher shall entrust this task only to a translator who is *familiar with classical French* (that is to say, with books published before 1940) and who, in addition, is regarded as a good prose-writer in his or her own language. Failing which, it would be better to leave it to another publisher to bring the project to a successful conclusion at a later date when conditions are right. The translator who is booked according to such criteria must then submit to the author a draft translation of the following passages:*

Pages 15–16. From 'Ma méthode ...' to: 'l'ancienne société.'

Pages 47–48. From 'La majorité des vins ...' to: 'avante le buveur.'

Pages 69–70. From 'Je me suis beaucoup intéressé . . .' to: 'je laisserai d'autres conclure.'

Pages 82–83. From 'Les plaisirs de l'existence ...' to: 'le soupçonner d'être passéiste.'

It will furthermore be necessary to have translated the aforementioned sentence from page 40: 'Entre la rue du Four et la rue de Buci ...'

Those who have satisfied these demands may subesquently, of course, ask the author for any additional explanation they might regard as desirable in order to understand a few other points.

III

The meaning of the passage written in the Coquillards' jargon (pages 24–25) follows here:

*Page numbers here follow the 1993 Gallimard edition – *Trans.*

'There I knew a few faces the executioner was waiting for: thieves and murderers. They were pals you could trust, for they never hesitated when it came to resorting to force. They were often picked up by the police, but they were good at feigning innocence and mis-leading them. That's where I learned how to deceive interrogators, so that long after and even now, I'd rather remain silent about such business. Our acts of violence and our earthly delights are past. And yet I vividly recall my penniless comrades who understood so well this delusory world: when all of us met up in our regular hangouts, in Paris at night.'

When translated into Spanish, this passage should be rendered in *germanía* (or perhaps *caló*). When translated into English, cant should be used. A German translation should use *Rotwelsch*. An Italian one should resort to *furbesco*. In view of these requirements, the translator may seek the aid of a specialist.

IV

As for the quotations whose authorship has not been given, there now follows a list of them in the order in which they appear in the text:

Page 7: Cardinal de Retz. Page 23: Queen Anne of Austria; the sentence 'The spirit whirleth …

PANEGYRIC 2

thither they return again' is a paraphrase of Eccle-
siastes. Page 25: a seventeenth-century popular song;
a proverb from the Auvergne. Page 34: a brief allusion
to the poet Nicolas Gilbert. Page 37: Machiavelli in a
letter to Vettori dated 10 December 1513. Page 41:
Dante in Italian; a quotation from the Bible (Psalm
39:12–13); a song from Asturias. Page 44: a frequent
image in Chinese poetry. Page 51: both quotations are
from Pascal. Page 56: Vauvenargues. Pages 56–57: a
fifteenth-century chronicler. Page 57: the first quotation comes from Charles d'Orléans, the second from
the King of England, William of Orange. Page 66: here
another quotation from the Bible is reversed ('Wis-
dom hath builded her house . . .' Proverbs 9). The
quotation on pages 66–67 is from Guy Debord (thesis
46 of *The Society of the Spectacle*). The last sentence
of the book is the traditional form of conclusion used
by the Spanish authors of the *Siglo de Oro*.

It is assumed that the quotations from identi-
fied authors will not pose any special problems
and will be fairly easy to locate. It will, of course,
be imperative to quote them in the original
whenever they issue from the same language into
which the book is to be translated. Otherwise, it
will at the very least be necessary to use these
quotations in translations that may already exist in
the foreign country, if they are considered truly
authoritative (which is the case, for example,

177

with the *early* German or English adaptations of the Bible). However, in the case where other translations, of more recent date, appear bad or simply mediocre, they would obviously have to be improved upon or else entirely rewritten.

November 1989)

Editor's note

Well-informed readers will now be able to judge the acceptability or otherwise of all the translations of *Panégyrique* that have appeared to date, a list of which follows:

Germany (Tiamat)
Great Britain (Verso)
Greece (Eleuteros Typos)
Italy (Castelvecchi)
Portugal (Antigona)

Note for the printer

The documents numbered from 1 to 57 must go across the entire page: thus 28 picas (12.5 cm). Some will run full page; others will run only the width of the page.

The documents lettered A to J should be 15 picas high (6.75 cm).

The documents K and L, 20 picas wide (9 cm).

The dates: 1951
            1953
            1958
            1968
            1977
            1984   must be set thus: **1937**

Each of these numbers 1, 2, 3, 4, 5, and 6 should be 30 mm high.

The words AUTHOR'S NOTE should be set thus:

STATI

Pagination, where feasible: at the bottom of the page.

G. D.

Les documents marqués de 1 à 57 doivent tenir toute la largeur de la page : donc 28 ciceros. Certains seront en pleine page ; d'autres en sortiront par trois côtés.

Les documents marqués de A à J auront une largeur de 15 ciceros. *6,75 cm*

Les documents K et L, une largeur de 20 ciceros. *9 cm*

Il faut composer les dates de : 1951
                                1953
                                1958
                                1968
                                1977
                                1984   ainsi : 1937

Avoir les chiffres 1, 2, 3, 4, 5, et 6 : chacun sur une hauteur de 30 m/m.

Le mot AVIS sera composé ainsi : STATI

La pagination possible : en bas de page.

G. D.

Facsimile of 'Note for the printer'.

Printed in the United States
by Baker & Taylor Publisher Services